GREAT AFRICAN AMERICANS IN

The Arts

CARLOTTA HACKER

Crabtree Publishing Company

Dedication

This series is dedicated to the African-American men and women who followed their dreams. With courage, faith, and hard work, they overcame obstacles in their lives and went on to excel in their fields. They set standards as some of the best Olympic athletes in the world. They brought innovation to film, jazz, and the arts, and the world is richer for their touch. They became leaders, and through their example encouraged hope and self-reliance. *Outstanding African Americans* is both an acknowledgment of and a tribute to these people.

Project Manager
Lauri Seidlitz

Production Manager
Amanda Howard

Editor
Virginia Mainprize

Copy Editor
Janice Parker

Design
Warren Clark

Layout
Chris Bowerman

Photograph Credits

Cover: Allen photo (Photofest), Parks photo (Globe Photos: Adam Scull), Torrence photo (Irene Young); **Dr. Rae Alexander-Minter:** pages 40, 41; **Archive Photos:** page 30; **Archives of American Art, Smithsonian Institution:** pages 42, 44, 45, 52; **Canapress Photo Service:** page 37; **Globe Photos:** pages 4, 9 (Stephen Allan), 10 (Tom Rodriguez), 13 (Christine Loss), 14 (Donald Sanders), 15 (Michael Ferguson), 21 (Hy Simon), 28 (Adam Scull), 32 (Walter Weissman), 49 (Ralph Dominguez), 7, 33; **Flora Roberts, Inc.:** page 46; **Collection of the Newark Museum, Gift of Mr. and Mrs. Henry H. Wehrhane, 1929:** page 43; **Northwestern State University of Louisiana, Watson Memorial Library, Cammie G. Henry Research Center:** pages 23 (Bailey Collection Scrapbook #1), 24 (Francois Mignon), 27 (Bailey Collection Scrapbook #4), 22, 25, 26; **Photofest:** pages 35 (Martha Swope), 38 (Don Perdue), 55 (Edward Steichen), 5, 12; **Schomburg Center for Research in Black Culture, New York Public Library:** pages 6 (Carl Van Vechten), 16, 17, 19, 31; **Jeffrey St. Mary:** page 34; **Urban Archives, Temple University, Philadelphia, Pennsylvania:** page 11 (David Powers); **UPI/Corbis-Bettmann:** pages 8, 61 (Richard Harbus), 18, 20, 29, 36, 39; **Irene Young:** page 58.

Every reasonable effort has been made to trace ownership and to obtain permission to reprint copyright material. The publishers would be pleased to have any errors or omissions brought to their attention so that they may be corrected in subsequent printings.

Published by
Crabtree Publishing Company

350 Fifth Avenue,	360 York Road, R.R. 4	73 Lime Walk
Suite 3308	Niagara-on-the-Lake	Headington
New York, NY	Ontario, Canada	Oxford OX3 7AD
U.S.A. 10018	L0S 1J0	United Kingdom

Cataloging-in-Publication Data

Hacker, Carlotta.
  Great African Americans in the arts / Carlotta Hacker.
    p.   cm. — (Outstanding African Americans)
  Includes index.
  Summary: Profiles thirteen African Americans from the fields of dance, stage, opera, classical music, photography, and painting.
    ISBN 0-86505-821-0 (pbk.). — ISBN 0-86505-807-5 (RLB)
  1. Afro-American artists—Biography—Juvenile literature. 2. Afro-American arts—Juvenile literature. [1. Afro-Americans—Biography. 2. Artists. 3. Entertainers.]
I. Title. II. Series.
NX512.3.A35H3 1997
700'.92'396073—dc20
[B]   96-46676
                                                      CIP
                                                       AC

Contents

For other great African Americans in the arts, see the book

GREAT AFRICAN AMERICANS IN ENTERTAINMENT
Josephine Baker • Harry Belafonte • Sammy Davis, Jr. • Bill Cosby... and others!

Alvin Ailey

Personality Profile

Career: Dancer and choreographer.

Born: January 5, 1931, in Rogers, Texas, to Alvin and Lula Ailey.

Died: December 1, 1989, in New York City, New York.

Education: Thomas Jefferson High School, 1948; University of California at Los Angeles, 1949-51; Los Angeles City College, 1950-51; San Francisco State College, 1952-53; Lester Horton Dance Theater.

Awards: First prize at the Paris International Dance Festival, 1970; Spingarn Medal, National Association for the Advancement of Colored People (NAACP), 1976; Mayor's Award of Art and Culture, New York City, 1977; Samuel H. Scripps American Dance Festival Award, 1987; Lifetime Achievement Award, presented at Kennedy Center, 1988; and numerous honorary degrees.

Growing Up

When Alvin was a boy, tap dancing was all the rage. Movie stars such as Fred Astaire clicked away with heel and toe, looking very glamorous. There was hardly a child in America who did not try to copy them.

When Alvin's parents separated, his mother took him to Los Angeles, California. When he was in his teens, Alvin began taking tap-dancing lessons from a neighbor. A high school friend told Alvin about Lester Horton's school of modern dance in Hollywood where some of the best dancers in the country were trained.

Alvin attended Lester Horton's school but dropped out after a month. He loved dancing but thought a teaching career would be more secure. "I didn't really see myself as a dancer," he later wrote. "I mean, what would I dance? It was 1949. A man didn't just become a dancer. Especially a black man."

For the next few years, Alvin went to college and studied languages. However, he attended Saturday classes at Lester's school. Soon, he realized that this was where he belonged. He was happiest when he was dancing.

"I enjoy most making a thing, to see it suddenly exist where nothing was before."

Alvin as a child in Texas.

Developing Skills

I n 1953, Alvin decided he was definitely going to be a dancer. Once again, he joined the Lester Horton Dance Theater. That winter, Lester had a heart attack and died. To keep the company going, Alvin took over Lester's role as choreographer. A choreographer is the person who creates or arranges dances, working out the steps and movements.

Alvin thought it would be more practical to be a teacher, but he was happiest when he was dancing.

The following year, Alvin was invited to New York City to dance in the musical *House of Flowers*. He stayed in New York, and during the next few years, he performed in several ballets and musicals. Meanwhile, he studied modern dance, ballet, and acting. With expert training and several years of experience, he became a brilliant dancer. In 1957, he was given a leading role in the musical *Jamaica*.

In 1958, Alvin formed his own dance group of eight black dancers, the Alvin Ailey American Dance Theater. His aim was to promote African-American music and culture. His most famous work, *Revelations*, was based on African-American religious music.

Alvin performed dances by other choreographers as well as his own pieces. He also began to include white dancers in his group. In 1964, he took the company on its first European tour. They created a sensation wherever they performed. At the end of a performance in Hamburg, Germany, the curtain was raised sixty-one times before the audience would stop clapping.

Because he had gained too much weight, Alvin had to stop performing as a dancer in 1965. He continued to choreograph and direct, and he spent more time teaching. In 1971, he opened a dance school, the Alvin Ailey American Dance Center. During the 1970s, he also did more touring. The U.S. State Department sent his company on a series of world tours to forty-four countries.

By the end of his life, Alvin had achieved far more than he had planned when he set out to promote African-American dance as an art form. He had not only made modern African-American dance a central part of American culture, but he had also made it famous throughout the world.

Alvin's dance company included both black and white dancers.

Accomplishments

1950 First joined Lester Horton's company on a regular basis.

1953 Became director of the company when Lester died.

1954 Moved to New York City to dance in musicals and ballets.

1958 Formed the Alvin Ailey American Dance Theater.

1960 Created and produced *Revelations*.

1964 Took his dance group on its first European tour.

1971 Opened the Alvin Ailey American Dance Center.

1974 Staged *Night Creature*.

Overcoming Obstacles

Even though Alvin's company was so successful, he often had money problems. Most dance companies need grants of money from the government or other sources to help them keep going. They seldom make enough just from ticket sales, even when they are playing to a full house.

Alvin did get some support. From 1966 on, the National Council on the Arts provided him with grants. In the 1970s, the U.S. State Department helped fund his world tours. Even so, money was always a worry. Sometimes, Alvin would choreograph a ballet for a producer just so that he could get the funds to pay his company's phone bill.

Alvin helped people who were blind learn to dance.

Eventually, the stress became too much for Alvin. As well as trying to make ends meet, he was doing too many different things. In 1980, he had a nervous breakdown. He was in the hospital for several weeks. When he recovered, he resolved to take life more easily. "Give up something. Do less. Concentrate on what's really important," he told an interviewer.

In fact, Alvin had spent his whole life concentrating on what was really important. Through his efforts, he had brought African-American culture to the world. His dances feature many aspects of this culture, including jazz, the blues, and spirituals. Some of his pieces honor individual African-American musicians. His 1974 production of *Night Creature* was a tribute to the famous bandleader Duke Ellington.

Alvin received many honors as he grew older. In 1979, New York City held a special Alvin Ailey American Dance Theater Twentieth Anniversary Day. He also received numerous honorary degrees and "lifetime achievement" awards. One such award was presented to Alvin at the Kennedy Center just one year before his death.

Special Interests

- Alvin was interested in all the arts and was a keen reader.
- Alvin liked to travel and learn about the dance forms of other countries.

Debbie Allen

Personality Profile

Career: Dancer, singer, actor, and television producer.

Born: January 16, 1950, in Houston, Texas, to Andrew and Vivian Allen.

Family: Married Winfred Wilford, 1975, (divorced, 1983); married Norman Nixon, 1984. Has two children, Vivian and Norman.

Education: Ballet Nacional de México; Houston Foundation for Ballet; B.A., Howard University, 1971.

Awards: Three Emmy awards for choreography for "Fame," 1982-87; Tony award, 1986; star on the Hollywood Walk of Fame, 1991; *Essence* award, 1992.

Growing Up

All of Debbie's family were talented. Her mother was a famous poet. Her father was a dentist. One of her brothers became a jazz musician, and her sister, Phylicia Rashad, became a well-known actor on "The Cosby Show."

Debbie in 1978, rehearsing with Thomas Pinnock (left) and Jeffrey Anderson-Gunter.

Debbie also became an actor, but her first ambition was to be a dancer. She started dancing lessons when she was three. In 1958, when Debbie was eight, her mother hired a ballet dancer from the Ballet Russe to teach her. Later, her mother took her oldest children to Mexico so that Debbie could train at Mexico's national ballet school. There, she not only studied dancing but also learned to speak Spanish.

When Debbie returned to Houston at the age of fourteen, she was dancing so well that she won a scholarship to the Houston Foundation for Ballet. Debbie was the only black dancer in this group. At high school, Debbie's friends called her Miss Versatile because she was good at so many different things. Debbie hoped to continue studying dance at the North Carolina School of the Arts but was refused admission. She completed her education at Howard University in Washington, D.C., where she studied speech and theater arts.

"Growing up in a place where you could see the sun, the sky, and have a lot of trees and grass, you felt like you really had a place in this universe."

Developing Skills

After graduating from Howard University, Debbie moved to New York City. In 1972, she landed a small part dancing in the musical *Purlie*. She continued to study dance and in 1973, was given the lead role in the musical *Raisin.* In 1975, Debbie began to perform on television. Her first roles were in commercials. Debbie and her sister worked together in an advertisement for disposable diapers. It was not the great dramatic role Debbie had dreamed of, but it was a start.

During the next few years, Debbie landed better parts, but she had to work very hard to get them. To prepare for a leading role in the play *Anna Lucasta*, she rehearsed up to twelve hours a day for three weeks—and then the play ran for only two weekends. Meanwhile, Debbie was getting more television roles, and in 1979, she appeared in her first movie, *The Fish That Saved Pittsburgh.*

Debbie starred in the hit television series "Fame."

Debbie's big break came in 1980 when she played a leading part in the Broadway musical *West Side Story*. The critics raved about her performance, but that was nothing compared to their praise for her next role. Debbie had a tiny part as a dancing teacher in the movie *Fame*. She had only two lines to speak, yet she spoke them with such impact that she was offered a role when the movie became a television series.

Fame was made into a television series that ran for several years. As well as acting in the show, Debbie created dances for it and directed several episodes. She often arrived at the studio at six in the morning to start working on the dances.

By the time the series ended in 1987, Debbie was an experienced television director. She produced "The Debbie Allen Special" in 1988. That year, she also became director and producer of the series "A Different World."

Debbie has since directed and performed in many more television shows, including the made-for-television movie "Stompin' at the Savoy." From 1991 to 1994, she created the dances for the Academy Awards ceremony. As if all this were not enough, Debbie has also recorded an album, *Special Look*.

Debbie is a star on stage and television and in the movies.

Accomplishments

1972 Danced in *Purlie*.

1975 Acted in television commercials.

1977 Performed in her first television series, "3 Girls 3."

1979 Appeared in her first movie, *The Fish That Saved Pittsburgh*.

1980 Played in the Broadway musical *West Side Story* and in the movie *Fame*.

1982-87 Choreographer, director, dancer, and actress in the television series "Fame."

1988 Produced "The Debbie Allen Special" for ABC-TV.

1988-92 Director of the television series "A Different World."

1989 Released first album, *Special Look*.

1991-94 Choreographer of the Academy Awards ceremonies.

"As soon as I've done something once, I'm anxious to try it out again and see where that leads me."

When people ask Debbie about her success, she often mentions her childhood in Texas. Even though her parents separated when she was seven, she had a happy home life and received plenty of praise. Yet, things were not as perfect as they seemed.

When Debbie was growing up, there was a lot of racism in Texas. African Americans were not allowed in most movie theaters or amusement parks. When Debbie first tried to enroll at the Houston Foundation for Ballet, she was rejected. That was why her mother hired a private ballet teacher for Debbie when she was eight. When she was finally accepted at age fourteen, she was the only black person in the dance company.

As Debbie grew up, the civil rights movement worked to end unequal treatment of African Americans. Even so, Debbie was not accepted when, in her late teens, she applied to the North Carolina School of the Arts. The dance director there told her she was "built wrong." Debbie thought this meant that she was built "the wrong color." She was so upset that she decided to give up dancing.

Instead, Debbie decided to go to Howard University where she studied speech and theater arts. She thought she might become a teacher. During her first year at Howard University, Debbie did not dance at all. Then a friend asked her to join his dance group, and soon Debbie was dancing in many student productions.

From then on, Debbie never looked back. She proved she was not "built wrong" for anything. Sometimes there were disappointments, but determination was the key to Debbie's success. "Nothing is simple," she says. She knows that if you want to do something well, you have to work at it.

To show their appreciation of Debbie's work, some colleges have given her honorary degrees. One college that recognized her success in this way in the early 1990s was the North Carolina School of the Arts. This was the college that had refused to have Debbie as a dance student twenty-five years earlier.

Debbie with her family as she received a star on the Hollywood Walk of Fame.

Special Interests

- Debbie has always been interested in teaching. When she was at Howard University, she gave children dancing lessons. In 1993, she became a member of the executive committee of the theater school at the University of California at Los Angeles.
- Debbie says she has two other favorite roles: being the wife of NBA all-star Norman Nixon and the mother of their children.

Marian Anderson

Personality Profile

Career: Singer.

Born: February 17, 1902, in Philadelphia, Pennsylvania, to John and Anna Anderson.

Died: April 8, 1993, in Portland, Oregon.

Family: Married Orpheus Fisher, 1943.

Education: William Penn High School; South Philadelphia High School for Girls; studied singing with Giuseppe Boghetti in the United States and with several teachers in Europe.

Awards: Julius Rosenwald Foundation award, 1931; Spingarn Medal, National Association for the Advancement of Colored People (NAACP), 1939; Bok Award, 1940; Presidential Medal of Freedom, 1963; Congressional Medal of Honor, 1977; Lifetime Achievement Award, presented at Kennedy Center, 1978; National Medal of Arts, 1986; Grammy Lifetime Achievement Award, 1991; medals from Finland, France, Haiti, Japan, Liberia, the Philippines, and Sweden; and twenty-four honorary degrees.

Growing Up

From her earliest years, Marian loved to sing and was never shy about performing in public. In 1908, when she was six, she joined the choir of her church. Two years later, she earned her first money as a singer. She was paid fifty cents for singing the hymn "The Lord Is My Shepherd."

Marian's father bought her a piano when she was eight. With no money for lessons, she taught herself how to play. She also ran errands and scrubbed floors to earn $3.45 to buy a violin from the local pawn shop. When Marian was twelve, her father died. She felt she should get a job to help her mother and her sisters, so she studied typing and shorthand at school. She joined the school choir, and her music teacher noticed her talent. She helped Marian transfer to another school that had an excellent music program.

Whenever she could take time from her schoolwork, Marian sang at local events to earn extra money for her family. She had an exceptionally beautiful voice. Yet, when she applied to the local music college, she was told, "We don't take African Americans."

Marian's mother told her not to give up and to pursue her dream of being a singer. Marian's school principal arranged for Marian to train with a famous voice teacher, Giuseppe Boghetti. Her church raised the money to pay for Marian's first year of training. Giuseppe was so impressed by Marian's voice that he taught her for free her second year.

"I dearly love the Negro spirituals. They are the unburdening of the sorrows of an entire race."

Giuseppe had never trained anyone with a voice as beautiful as Marian's. He taught Marian to use her voice like a musical instrument so that it was totally under her control. He also taught her to sing French, German, and Italian songs. Until then, she had usually sung hymns and spirituals. To be a concert singer, she would need a wide range of songs.

Marian in her opera debut with the Metropolitan Opera in New York City.

Marian gave her first concert to a mostly white audience in 1924. It was not a success. The reviewers criticized the way she pronounced foreign words. Marian seriously thought of giving up her musical career. Coached by Giuseppe, she improved her accent, and the following year, she won first prize among three hundred singers at a national singing contest. As the prize winner, Marian sang at a concert with the New York Philharmonic Orchestra. This time, reviewers went wild about her performance.

Despite this success, Marian's career was slow starting. She continued to sing mainly to black audiences who preferred to hear well-known spirituals rather than classical music. Marian realized that she would have to go to Europe if she wanted to succeed as a concert performer. She studied in England in 1929 and 1930, and in 1931, she went to Germany for training.

Marian spent many years studying singing in Europe.

Marian spent the next few years in Europe, studying singing and giving concerts. Audiences flocked to hear her sing both classical songs and spirituals. She sang for the kings of Sweden and Denmark and gave 108 concerts in twelve months.

By the time Marian returned to the United States in 1935, she was famous throughout Europe. Yet, she was little known at home. All this changed when she gave a concert at the Town Hall in New York City. She was a tremendous success. Everyone raved about her performance. The *New York Times* wrote that Marian was "one of the greatest singers of our time."

From then on, Marian was so busy that theaters had to book her two years in advance. She had become a major celebrity. She was invited to sing at the White House and sang at the inauguration of Presidents Eisenhower and Kennedy.

Accomplishments

1925 Won prize to sing with the New York Philharmonic Orchestra.

1931 Performed throughout Europe.

1935 Signed contract for performances in the United States.

1939 Performed at the Lincoln Memorial, Washington, D.C.

1955 Sang with the Metropolitan Opera, New York City.

1956 Published the book *My Lord, What a Morning*.

1958 Appointed U.S. delegate to the United Nations.

Overcoming Obstacles

Even after Marian had become a world-famous singer, she was still barred from entering some whites-only places in her own country. Marian hated touring in the United States. She had to travel in the black section of the train. She could not go to some restaurants or hotels. Despite her fame, many places were closed to her.

As Marian became more famous, she insisted that African Americans be admitted to all her concerts. She refused to sing for whites-only audiences. Yet, she still experienced racial prejudice. In 1939, the Daughters of the American Revolution would not let her sing in Constitution Hall in Washington, D.C. They owned the hall and said it was for whites only.

The First Lady, Eleanor Roosevelt, was furious when she heard about this. She arranged for Marian to give a free outdoor concert at the Lincoln Memorial in Washington. The concert was held on Easter Sunday, 1939. More than 75,000 people came to hear Marian on that chilly April morning. Millions more listened to her on radio.

Marian singing at the Lincoln Memorial in 1939.

Standing in front of the statue of Abraham Lincoln, Marian began her performance by singing "My Country 'Tis of Thee." She knew this concert was one of the most important in her life. She had become a symbol, representing all African Americans who were fighting for an equal place.

From then on, Marian had many concert offers, both at home and abroad. She could now charge very high fees, but she gave much of her earnings to charity. Meanwhile, she continued to lead the way for other black performers. In the 1930s, she had been the first African-American artist to sing at the White House. In 1955, she became the first to sing with the Metropolitan Opera in New York City.

Marian ended her career in 1965 with a worldwide concert tour ending in Carnegie Hall in New York City. Marian had achieved much more than she had ever dreamed of during her forty-year career. As the Reverend Jesse Jackson said, "Beyond her extraordinary singing powers, she was a source of light and hope in one of the dark periods of American history."

Marian in 1980.

Special Interests

- Marian was concerned about poverty in the world. She helped found the Freedom from Hunger Foundation.
- Marian was always ready to give a helping hand to those starting in music. In 1941, she set up a scholarship for young singers.

Clementine Hunter

Growing Up

Clementine was born in 1886 at Hidden Hill, a cotton plantation in Louisiana. She spent her childhood and the early part of her adult life picking cotton. For a short time, she attended a nearby school. Then her family moved to another plantation—the Melrose Plantation near Natchitoches, Louisiana. Clementine never went to school again. Although she lived to be 101, she never learned to read.

Clementine did not begin her career as an artist until she was fifty-three years old.

All day, Clementine was busy in the cotton fields. Later, after she married, she was even busier. She had two children by her first marriage and five more by her second marriage. Looking after her large family and picking cotton all day was a lot of work. When she was in her thirties Clementine finally got an easier job. She became a domestic servant to the family who owned the Melrose Plantation.

Working in the house instead of the fields gave Clementine a chance to try out her sewing skills. Saving up small, left-over scraps of material, she began making quilts. The plantation owner was interested in arts and crafts, and she encouraged Clementine to make quilts and baskets in her spare time. The more Clementine made, the more she enjoyed designing them. She believed she would be good at other forms of art too. All she needed was the chance to show what she could do.

Developing Skills

T he plantation owner had a big art collection, and in 1939, she hired a French writer, François Mignon, to look after it. One evening, Clementine came to François with some nearly empty tubes of paint that had been thrown away by an artist who was visiting the plantation. She told François she wanted to try and "mark" a painting just like the artist. François found her an old window shade to use as a canvas.

Early the next morning, Clementine showed François the picture she had painted during the night. This was the first picture she showed to anyone other than her family. She was fifty-three years old. François encouraged her to paint more. She began to paint on all sorts of things—paper bags, used bottles, cardboard boxes, and iron pots. François made sure Clementine always had a good supply of oil paints because she could not afford to buy them herself.

Once Clementine began to sell her works, she was able to buy her own paints as well as proper artists' canvas. Before long, she was a well-known artist. In 1949, some of Clementine's paintings were shown in the New Orleans Arts and Crafts show. Then in 1955, the Delgado Museum in New Orleans gave an exhibition of her work. This was the first exhibition the museum had ever given for an African-American artist.

In 1956, when she was seventy, Clementine painted one of her most famous works. There was a traditional African-style house on the Melrose property. François suggested that Clementine paint wood panels for the house. She painted nine murals, each with a different scene showing life on the plantation. She also painted some smaller panels to go between the big ones. Clementine later painted similar murals for two other buildings at Melrose.

Clementine's work became popular with big-city art galleries and was shown at important museums. She sold many of her paintings, but mostly to friends for small sums. Even so, she made enough money to buy herself a trailer. There she lived happily, just a few miles from Melrose, during the last years of her long life. She continued painting until a month before she died. She had painted more than five thousand pieces.

Clementine with some of her paintings.

Accomplishments

1940 Painted her first picture.

1949 Featured in the New Orleans Arts and Crafts show.

1955 Work exhibited by Delgado Museum, New Orleans, and by Northwestern State College, Natchitoches.

1956 Painted murals for African House.

1973 Work exhibited at the Museum of American Folk Art, New York City.

1974 Gave a one-person show at Fisk University.

1985 Work included in the Twentieth-Century American Folk Art exhibition, University of Santa Clara, California.

C lementine started out with little money, no education, and no training. Hard work and few rewards—that was the type of life she expected. And that was the type of life Clementine had for her first fifty years.

Until she was almost thirty-five, Clementine picked cotton. Only when she became a servant at Melrose Plantation did she have a chance to try her artistic skills. She began making quilts that soon became works of art.

By the 1970s, other artists were painting forgeries of her work, trying to sell them as originals.

Clementine was over fifty when she began her career as a painter. She might never have begun at all if she had not asked François for help. She was sure she had talent, and she wanted to prove it.

Clementine did three main types of painting. Most common were her "memory" paintings because she preferred to paint from memory than from real life. These were scenes of everyday life, such as cooking food, washing clothes, playing games, and going to a wedding. The second type was based on stories from the Bible. In these paintings, all the people and angels are always black. The third type of painting was abstracts. An art expert, who considered Clementine "almost a genius," suggested that she try this style. He made paste-up collages from magazines and showed them to Clementine. She began painting her own pattern pictures, using even brighter colors than before.

More and more people began to recognize Clementine's rare talent. In 1959, Northwestern State College in Natchitoches held a special exhibition of Clementine's work. But Clementine was not allowed to view it at the same time as the white visitors. She was let in the back door after the gallery had closed.

By the 1970s, Clementine had become very famous. There were television programs about her paintings, and she had many showings of her work. One of the most important was an exhibition in Washington, D.C. By this time, Clementine no longer had to creep in the back door. For her Washington exhibition, President Carter sent her a personal invitation. But Clementine was not impressed. "If Jimmy Carter wants to see me," she said, "he knows where I am. He can come here." Clementine was not a traveler. She lived and died in Louisiana. Today, her fame has spread from coast to coast across America.

Clementine lived to be 101 years old.

Special Interests

- Clementine's chief interest was the plantation life she had known for so long. It was the subject of much of her art.

Gordon Parks

Personality Profile

Career: Photographer, film director, and author.

Born: November 30, 1912, in Fort Scott, Kansas, to Andrew and Sarah Parks.

Family: Married Sally Alvis, 1933, (divorced, 1961); married Elizabeth Campbell, 1962, (divorced, 1973); married Genevieve Young, 1973, (divorced, 1979). Has three children by his first marriage, Gordon, Jr., Toni, and David; and one child by his second marriage, Leslie.

Awards: Julius Rosenwald Foundation grant, 1942; Notable Book Award from the American Library Association, 1966; Emmy award, 1968; Spingarn Medal, National Association for the Advancement of Colored People (NAACP), 1972; Christopher Award, 1978; National Medal of Arts, 1988; Paul Robeson Award from the Black Filmmakers Hall of Fame; and many other awards and honors.

Growing Up

Gordon was the youngest in a family of fifteen children. He was raised in Fort Smith, Kansas, a city where African Americans were given a hard time. Gordon's mother told him he must never think he was not as good as whites. "If a white boy can do it, so can you," she told him. "So don't ever give me your color as a cause for failing."

Despite the racism in Fort Smith, Gordon had a happy childhood. But in 1927, when he was fifteen, his mother died. Gordon was shattered. He had loved her very much. He was sent to live with a married sister and her husband in St. Paul, Minnesota. This was not a good arrangement. Gordon's brother-in-law did not like having him there, and one night he threw Gordon out of the house.

It was the middle of winter and Gordon found himself out on the streets. He had no money, and he was all alone. During the next few months, he took whatever jobs he could get—mopping floors or washing dishes. At night, he rode the streetcars to keep warm. He had to drop out of school, but he tried to keep up his education by reading in the public library whenever he had the time.

B y 1934, Gordon had a steady job with the Northern Pacific Railroad. He was a waiter in the dining car. One day, he picked up a magazine that had been left on a seat. It was full of photographs of farm workers. As Gordon looked at the photos, he realized how much a picture can say about people. Then and there, he decided to become a photographer.

Gordon directed the film version of his novel **The Learning Tree.**

Gordon bought a second-hand camera and taught himself how to take and develop photographs. As he traveled back and forth on the railroad, he saw many scenes he wanted to record. Most of his photos were of ordinary African Americans going about their daily lives in the big cities. This was what interested Gordon most. He wanted to tell the world about the difficult lives of low-income African Americans.

One way or another, Gordon has been doing this ever since. He started with a series of photos about the Chicago slums. They were so powerful that they got him a job as a photographer with the U.S. Farm Security Administration (FSA). Some of America's best photographers worked for the FSA, and Gordon learned a lot while working with them. He later spent twenty years producing photo stories for *Life* magazine. As a staff photographer for *Life*, Gordon's photos were seen by people all over the world.

In the 1960s, Gordon tried his hand at other media. First, he wrote a novel, *The Learning Tree*. It was about a black family in Kansas. Like his photos, it portrayed the sufferings of African Americans, and it also showed their strength and dignity. In 1968, *The Learning Tree* was made into a movie by Warner Brothers, a major Hollywood film company. Gordon directed the film himself. It was the first time Warner Brothers had hired an African-American director.

Since then, Gordon has directed more films and written more books, including a book of poetry. One of his best-known films is *Martin*. It is a ballet about the civil rights leader Martin Luther King, Jr. *Martin* was shown on PBS television in 1990.

Gordon worked for equality for minorities through his film, photography, and writing.

Accomplishments

1937-42 Freelance photographer.

1942-43 Staff photographer with the U.S. Farm Security Administration.

1944 War correspondent with the U.S. Office of War Information.

1945-48 Photographer for Standard Oil, New Jersey.

1948-68 Photojournalist with *Life* magazine.

1963 Published *The Learning Tree*.

1968 Directed movie version of *The Learning Tree*.

1970 Founded *Essence* magazine.

1990 His ballet *Martin* was shown on television.

During his early years, Gordon often had to deal with racial insults. Like other African Americans, he was treated as a second-class citizen. But unlike many, he found a way of fighting back. Gordon used his camera as a weapon. With it, he took pictures that shocked people and made them see how unfair life was for blacks in the United States. In this way, he waged his own war against racism.

Gordon took one of his most famous photos the day he arrived in Washington, D.C., to work for the FSA. He was in a furious temper because of what had just happened to him. He had gone to get a quick lunch in a drugstore and had been told it was for whites only. The same thing had happened when he tried to get served in a department store. The photo Gordon took that day said a lot about the way America treated its black citizens. The photo is of a black woman who had mopped floors for the government all her life. Holding her mop and broom, she is standing in front of the American flag.

"The first black this, the first black that. I don't appreciate that as much as people think I do. I have no doubt there were other blacks who could have done it just as well or a lot better."

Gordon took many similar photos during his year with the FSA during World War II. He then became a war correspondent—but not for long. He wanted to do a photo story about an all-black squadron of fighter pilots, but he was not allowed to go overseas to take pictures of them. Angrily, Gordon quit. He then tried to get a job as a fashion photographer with *Harper's Bazaar*. Again, the fact that he was African American stood in his way. The magazine would not hire a black photographer.

Harper's was soon to regret this decision. Gordon was hired by two other top fashion magazines and later by *Life* magazine. As a black photographer working for *Life* in the 1960s, Gordon played a very important role in the fight to get equal treatment for blacks. He showed the world the civil rights movement from an African-American point of view. Some of his most powerful photos against racism were taken at this time.

Gordon with his son Gordon Jr. and friend Maybelle Ley Marie.

In his fight against racism, Gordon achieved many firsts. He was the first black photographer to work for such major magazines as *Vogue* and *Life*. He was the first African American to work for the U.S. Farm Security Administration and the Office of War Information. He was the first African American to become a leading filmmaker in Hollywood. Because of his efforts, the doors to these professions were opened to other black Americans.

Special Interests

- Gordon was very fond of music. He played the piano well and composed several musical works, including *Piano Concerto* (1953) and *Tree Symphony* (1967).
- Gordon helped a sick Brazilian boy called Flavio whom he met when doing a photo story in Brazil. Gordon brought Flavio to a clinic in the United States so he could be cured. Gordon's first documentary film was about Flavio.

Ntozake Shange

Personality Profile

Career: Playwright and poet.

Born: October 18, 1948, in Trenton, New Jersey, to Paul and Eloise Williams.

Family: Married twice; second marriage to David Murray, 1977, (divorced). Has one daughter, Savannah.

Education: B.A. (*cum laude*), Barnard College, New York, 1970; M.A., University of Southern California at Los Angeles, 1973.

Awards: Obie award for best play, 1977, 1981; Outer Critics Circle Award, 1977; Audelco Award, 1977; *Mademoiselle* Award, 1977; Frank Silvera Writer's Workshop Award, 1978; Los Angeles book prize for poetry, 1981; Excellence Medal, Columbia University, 1981; Guggenheim fellowship, 1981; Taos World Heavyweight Poetry Champion, 1992, 1993, 1994.

Growing Up

N tozake Shange is an African name. In the Zulu language, Ntozake means "she who comes with her own things," and Shange means "one who walks with the lion." Ntozake (pronounced En-to-za-key) chose the name for herself in 1971. Before that, she was called Paulette Williams after her father, air force surgeon Paul Williams.

The eldest of four children, Ntozake grew up in a cultured home filled with music, dance, and literature. Her mother was a social worker and teacher who read stories to her children and encouraged them to write their own. On Sunday afternoons, the family often staged variety shows—dancing, singing, and reciting poetry.

Life became even more artistic in the mid-1950s when the family moved to St. Louis, Missouri. Many of the city's jazz musicians and writers became friends of Ntozake's parents, and they often visited. There was always something exciting going on or somebody exciting to talk to in the Williams's home. Yet this was a difficult time for Ntozake. She was bussed to a German-American school where the other students picked on her. Ntozake was glad when she was thirteen and her family moved back to New Jersey.

Ntozake attended high school in New Jersey and then studied for a bachelor's degree at Barnard College in New York. She completed her education by earning a master's degree at the University of Southern California at Los Angeles in 1973.

"There was always different music at our house all the time."

Developing Skills

After university, Ntozake taught for two years at Sonoma State College and Mills College in California. She was a very angry young woman at the time. She had been angry about racism ever since attending school in St. Louis.

Ntozake was also angry about the way women were treated by men. She had married young and was separated from her husband. Almost all of Ntozake's books and plays are about the problems faced by black women.

Ntozake began writing about these problems while she was teaching. She was also involved with poetry and dance groups. She formed her own dance company, which she called For Colored Girls Who Have Considered Suicide. This was also the name of Ntozake's first major dance show.

In 1975, Ntozake moved her dance company to New York City. There they performed *For Colored Girls* in a loft where jazz groups usually played. Before long, a director saw the show, thought it was extremely good, and moved it to a theater. By 1976, it was playing on Broadway.

Ntozake, on the right, in her play **For Colored Girls Who Have Considered Suicide.** *It was reviewed as "a searing, joyful, wonderful tribute to black women in America."*

The show was highly original. Ntozake called it a "choreopoem" because it was a mixture of dance, poetry, and music. *For Colored Girls* made people realize just how much African-American women have suffered over the years, and it honored those who have refused to give up hope. It was a very powerful work. After playing in New York, it went on tour through the United States and overseas. In 1977, the show won Ntozake an Obie award, the Outer Critics Circle Award, an Audelco Award, and the *Mademoiselle* Award.

Ntozake won another Obie award in 1981 for her play *Mother Courage and Her Children*. Meanwhile, *For Colored Girls* continued to be an outstanding success. It was shown on PBS television in 1982.

"I live in language—sound falls round me like rain on other folks."

Accomplishments

1975 Put on first performance of *For Colored Girls*.

1976 Published her first novel, *Sassafrass*.

1977 Published her first poetry book, *Natural Disasters and Other Festive Occasions*.

1980 First performance of the play *Mother Courage and Her Children*.

1981 Published a prize-winning book of poems, *Three Pieces*.

1985 Published the novel *Betsey Brown*.

1995 Was keynote speaker at the Black Arts and Sciences Festival.

1996 Delivered the Martin Luther King, Jr., Memorial Lecture at Wellesley College.

Ntozake had a special reason for including the word "suicide" in the title of *For Colored Girls*. After her separation from her first husband when she was not yet twenty, she felt such despair that she tried to kill herself. On one occasion, she put her head in a gas oven. Another time, she took an overdose of pills. She slashed her wrists, drank chemicals, and tried to drive her car into the Pacific Ocean.

Finally, Ntozake realized this was not the way to solve her problems. It would be far better to write about them—to write about the problems all African-American women face. That way, she could draw attention to them. As well, she could give other women encouragement so that they would not give up hope. This is what she was doing when she wrote *For Colored Girls* and what she has been doing ever since.

Ntozake has produced a vast amount of work: more than a dozen plays and "choreopoems," an operetta, novels, and numerous books of poetry and essays. The main theme in all her works is the abuse that women and children suffer. Her message is that people should not put up with suffering. They must keep trying and must help others who are struggling to cope. Her work encourages people to refuse despair.

Ntozake used many of her own experiences to write her plays.

As well as writing all these works and often performing in them as well, Ntozake has taught and lectured at many universities. In 1996, she was the Mellon Distinguished Professor of Literature at Rice University. She was also the artist-in-residence at Villanova University and the writer-in-residence at the Maryland Institute College of Art. She likes teaching young people and is particularly interested in helping young women find a way of coping with the problems they will face in their lives.

Ntozake is shown here in 1976 with Melvin Van Peebles at the opening of her play **For Colored Girls.**

Special Interests

- Ntozake is fascinated by language and the way it is written. Sometimes she writes words the way they sound, such as writing "enuf" instead of "enough." She often shortens words and writes without capital letters, such as "our language shd let you know who's talkin, what we're talkin abt & how we cant stop sayin this."
- Ntozake cares a lot about young African-American women and tries to help them in every way possible.

Henry Ossawa Tanner

Personality Profile

Career: Painter.

Born: June 21, 1859, in Pittsburgh, Pennsylvania, to Benjamin and Sarah Tanner.

Died: May 25, 1937, in Paris, France.

Family: Married Jessie Olssen, 1899. Had one son, Jesse.

Education: Pennsylvania Academy of Fine Arts, 1880-1882; Academie Julien, Paris.

Awards: Numerous prizes and medals, including the silver medal at the Exposition Universelle, Paris, 1900; silver medal, Pan-American Exposition, Buffalo, 1904; silver medal, St. Louis Exposition, 1904; gold medal, Panama-Pacific Exposition, San Francisco, 1915; Legion of Honor, France, 1923.

Growing Up

When Henry was twelve, he saw an artist sketching in the local park. Henry watched, fascinated as the artist drew. Trees, grass, a big blue sky—it all looked so real. "It set me on fire," Henry later said. He knew that, above all else, he wanted to be a painter.

Henry borrowed fifteen cents from his mother to buy paints and brushes. Unlike many artists, Henry had parents who could afford to help him. The Tanners had a comfortable home in Philadelphia, Pennsylvania, where Henry's father was the rector of Bethel Church. Henry's parents were glad he had found a hobby that interested him.

The Tanner family around 1890. Left to right: Isabella, Halla, her daughter Sadie, Henry, Bishop Tanner, Carlton, Mrs. Tanner, Bertha, Sarah, and Mary.

As a teenager in the 1870s, Henry spent every spare moment sketching. Some of his pictures were landscapes. Others were of people or animals. Henry often visited the Philadelphia Zoo to practice drawing animals. One of his early paintings, *Pomp*, showed well-dressed people staring at a caged animal.

When Henry graduated from high school, he hoped to study at an art college. But his parents believed he should get a "real" job and keep painting as a hobby. Henry worked at a flour mill for a couple of years but had to stop when he became ill. His parents then let him pursue his dream of being an artist. In 1880, Henry enrolled at the Pennsylvania Academy of Fine Arts. When he left two years later, he was a skilled painter.

Developing Skills

I n the late nineteenth century, most American artists completed their training in Europe. Henry hoped to do so too. First, he had to save some money. Henry did not get to Europe until he was in his thirties.

Meanwhile, Henry produced some of his most notable work. Traveling in North Carolina, he sketched the people and countryside. From these sketches, he later did a series of paintings on African-American life.

Henry with the Old American Art Club in Paris, France. Henry is in the first row, fourth from the left.

Henry arrived in Europe in 1891. For the next five years, he was a student at one of the world's most famous art schools—the Academie Julien in Paris, France. During this time, Henry had his first big success. His painting *The Music Lesson* was included in the French Society of Artists' yearly show. Like many of his works, this painting was of an older person passing on skills to a younger person.

Two years later, Henry's *Daniel in the Lion's Den* won an honorable mention at the French Society of Artists' yearly show. This painting illustrated a story from the Bible, as did his next successful picture, *The Raising of Lazarus*. A wealthy American, who lived in Paris, was so impressed that he paid for Henry to go to Palestine and Egypt to paint more biblical pictures. Meanwhile, *The Raising of Lazarus* won a prize at the 1897 Paris Exhibition.

Henry decided to move to France. He had many friends in Paris, and he found far less racism there than in the United States. By the early 1900s, he was considered the leading American artist in Paris. In 1923, he received France's highest award, the Legion of Honor.

Henry was the first African-American artist to become famous in Europe and receive such honors. Equally important was the effect he had on American art. Most American artists were still trying to paint like the Europeans. They copied European methods because Europe was considered the true home of art. Henry painted in his own style, based on his own ideas. By doing so, he helped start a truly American form of painting.

Henry's painting
The Good Shepherd.

Accomplishments

1894 *The Music Lesson* was accepted by the French Society of Artists' show.

1896 *Daniel in the Lion's Den* won an honorable mention at the French Society of Artists' show.

1897 *The Raising of Lazarus* was bought by the French government.

1905 His paintings were included in the Carnegie Institute's exhibition.

1908 Held his first one-person show in New York.

1921 His works were included in the first large African-American art show in New York.

1922 A group of black artists in Washington, D.C., formed the Tanner Art League.

1923 Awarded the Legion of Honor by the French government.

1927 Elected a member of the American National Academy.

Overcoming Obstacles

I t is not easy to make a living as an artist. It takes time to become famous, and few artists earn enough money to live comfortably. Henry's parents knew that it would be especially difficult for an African American. That is why they tried to get him to choose another career.

Henry had a hard time selling his paintings at first. He could barely make enough to support himself. In 1888, he opened a photography studio in Atlanta, Georgia. He thought it might bring him a steady income, but it was not a success. Henry then took a teaching job at Clark University in Atlanta. There a friend of the family held an exhibition of Henry's pictures, hoping the public would buy some. Not even one painting was sold. The family friend then bought them all himself. This was how Henry got the money to go to France to study at the Academie Julien.

Henry as a lieutenant with the American Red Cross in France in 1918.

In France, Henry still found it hard to make a living as a painter. Although he won prizes for his pictures, he did not earn much money. Even so, he enjoyed himself. He painted all day long. He was happily married to a Swedish-born singer, and he was making a name for himself. In 1897, the French government bought one of his paintings. This was a great honor since the government had bought the works of only two other American artists before Henry.

In 1905, Henry was the first African American to be included in the Carnegie Institute's annual exhibition in New York City. American galleries began to buy his paintings, and in 1908, he had a one-person show in New York.

In spite of this success, the American art world did not claim Henry as a "great American artist." He was usually referred to as a "Negro artist." He was almost forgotten after his death. Not until the 1960s was Henry given his rightful place in American art history. In 1969, the Smithsonian Institution in Washington, D.C., put on an exhibition of his paintings. Since then, there have been other such shows, including one at the  Philadelphia Museum of Art in 1991. Henry is now considered a major figure in American art.

Special Interests

- As the son of a minister, Henry was very religious and liked to read the Bible. Many of his paintings illustrate stories from the Bible.
- Henry was an active member of the American art clubs in Paris. He enjoyed discussing ideas with his fellow artists.

Alice Childress

When Alice was five, her parents divorced, and she was sent to live with her grandmother in Harlem, New York. Alice's grandmother had little money but was wise and warm-hearted and loved her grand-daughter. To entertain Alice, she told her stories. She took Alice to museums and art galleries. Above all, she encouraged Alice to read. By the time Alice was a teenager, she had discovered the public library and was often reading two books a day.

Alice and her grandmother lived in one of the lowest-income parts of Harlem. As Alice was growing up, she heard about the problems of the people in her community. Many of the novels and plays that she later wrote were about such people. Alice once said that she chose to write about "ordinary" people "because they are not ordinary."

When she started working in her late teens, Alice met many other "ordinary" people. She had to leave school and get a job because her grandmother died. Alice worked in a factory and a store and in several other low-paying jobs. Meanwhile, she was hoping to become an actor.

In 1940, Alice landed her first acting role. It was in the play *On Strivers Row* which was performed by the American Negro Theater company in Harlem. For the next eleven years, Alice worked with this theater company. For the next eleven years, Alice worked with this company, writing, directing, and acting in plays. The first of her own plays to be performed was *Florence* in 1949. It was about a black woman and a white woman in a segregated railway waiting room.

In 1955, Alice wrote *Trouble in the Mind* which attracted a lot of notice and great praise. This very powerful play pointed out that white Americans have a mistaken view of African Americans. It won Alice an Obie award in 1956. Alice was the first African-American woman ever to win an Obie. In 1966, her next play, *Wedding Band*, attracted even more attention. It is about a love affair between a black woman and a white man. They hope to marry, but the laws of South Carolina at that time prevented marriage between blacks and whites. The play shocked many people when it was broadcast on television in 1973.

Personality Profile

Career: Playwright, novelist, and actor.

Born: October 12, 1920, in Charleston, South Carolina.

Education: Julia Ward Howe Junior High School; Wadleigh High School.

Awards: Obie award, 1956; *A Hero Ain't Nothin' but a Sandwich* was named one of the Outstanding Books of the Year by the *New York Times Book Review*, 1973; Paul Robeson Award, 1977; Black Filmmakers Hall of Fame Award, 1977; Radcliffe Graduate Society Medal, 1984; African Poets Theater Award, 1985; Harlem School of the Arts Humanitarian Award, 1987; honorary degree, New York State University, 1990; Langston Hughes Medal, 1995.

Alice has also written novels for young people. The best known is *A Hero Ain't Nothin' but a Sandwich*. This story is about a teenager who is hooked on drugs. It was banned by a school in Georgia, but it received high praise from most people and won several awards. The book was later made into a movie that also won many awards. Alice has since written several more scripts for movies and television.

For more than forty years, Alice has been giving the world a powerful picture of African-American life through her plays, "tele-plays," movie scripts, and books. She has also lectured at Fisk University and other colleges. Although Alice has worked in so many areas, she remains at heart a playwright. "The play form is the one most familiar to me and so influences all of my writing," she says. "I think in scenes."

Accomplishments

1940 Acted in *On Strivers Row*.

1949 Her play *Florence* was staged.

1955 First performance of *Trouble in the Mind*.

1966 Appointed lecturer at Fisk University.

1967 Was visiting scholar at the Radcliffe Institute for Independent Study.

1973 Published *A Hero Ain't Nothin' but a Sandwich*.

1975 Published *When the Rattlesnake Sounds*.

1987 Staged the play *Moms*.

1990 Published the young adults' novel *Those Other People*.

Katherine Dunham

Ever since she had stayed with her aunts as a small child, Katherine had wanted to be a dancer.

K atherine was only four years old when her mother died. The following year, in 1914, her father remarried and moved Katherine and her brother to Joliet, Illinois. There Katherine attended high school and later took dancing lessons at Joliet Junior College.

Ever since she had stayed with her aunts as a small child, Katherine had wanted to be a dancer. Her aunts had been rehearsing for a musical. Katherine thought it looked like fun. In her late teens, Katherine began to take dancing seriously. She enrolled at the University of Chicago to study modern dance and ballet.

To support herself as a student in Chicago, she and some friends started an African-American ballet group. This was a totally new idea. There were no black women ballet dancers at that time. Katherine's group attracted a lot of attention when it performed at the Chicago Beaux Arts Ball in 1931.

Meanwhile, Katherine was also becoming interested in anthropology—the study of social customs and their origins. She was fascinated by the role of dance in society and ceremony and was especially eager to learn about African-American dance forms.

For the next few years, Katherine studied anthropology at the University of Chicago. After earning her bachelor's degree in 1936, she began the research that led to an M.S. degree and then to a Ph.D. Katherine did her research in the West Indies. It seemed the best place to begin her study of the history of black dance. She hoped to trace many of the dances back to their roots in Africa.

Katherine did not have the money to pay for her travels herself, but she won two fellowships to support her studies. She went first to Jamaica where she stayed in an isolated village. After a while, the villagers came to trust her, and they let her watch some of their most secret dances. The same thing happened in Martinique, Trinidad, and Haiti. Katherine went several times to Haiti and was accepted into one of the secret dance societies there.

Personality Profile

Career: Dancer and anthropologist.

Born: June 22, 1909, in Chicago, Illinois, to Albert and Fanny Dunham.

Education: Joliet Junior College; B.A., University of Chicago, 1936; M.S., University of Chicago; Ph.D., Northwestern University.

Awards: Legion of Honor, Haiti; Julius Rosenwald Foundation award, 1939; *Dance* magazine Award, 1968; National Center of Afro-American Artists Award, 1972; American Dance Guild Award, 1975; Albert Schweitzer Music Award, 1979; Kennedy Center Award, 1983; National Medal of Arts, 1989; Capezio Dance Award, 1991.

Katherine visited other parts of the world, including Africa. Meanwhile, the effects of her research could be seen in her own dancing. She developed a new style that mixed ballet and modern dance with traditional West Indian dances and North American jazz. It was a stunning combination. Katherine and her company caused a sensation when they performed these dances. To teach her style to others, Katherine founded several dancing schools in the United States, as well as in France, Sweden, and Haiti. Visiting scholars and dancers came from Africa and Latin America.

In the 1960s, Katherine stopped performing as a dancer, but she remained active. When she was in her eighties, she was still conducting a children's workshop each year at the training center she had established in East St. Louis, Illinois.

Accomplishments

1931 Founded her first dancing school and dance company.

1939 Supervisor of the Chicago City Theater Project.

1943 Founded the Katherine Dunham School of Arts and Research, New York City. Appeared in the film *Stormy Weather*.

1959 Published her life story, *A Touch of Innocence*.

1961 Founded a dancing school in Haiti.

1966 Appointed artistic advisor to the President of Senegal.

1967 Founded the Performing Arts Training Center, East St. Louis, Illinois.

1968 Appointed professor at Southern Illinois University.

William Henry Johnson

William spent much of his childhood earning money to support his mother and his brothers and sisters. He seldom had time to go to school.

illiam was raised by his mother in South Carolina. He never knew his father who was white. William spent much of his childhood earning money to support his mother and his brothers and sisters. He seldom had time to go to school.

When William was seventeen, he moved to New York City. He was soon hard at work, doing whatever jobs he could get. This was an exciting time for African Americans in New York. Poets, writers, painters, and musicians were creating works of art based on their own experiences as African Americans. This period of artistic activity is known as the Harlem Renaissance, and soon William was part of it.

William became interested in art when he saw some cartoons in a local newspaper. This inspired him to do his own drawings, and in 1921, he enrolled at the National Academy of Design. During his five years there, he became one of the academy's top students.

During his summer vacations, William studied at the Cape Cod School of Art in Provincetown, Massachusetts. One of his instructors there was so impressed by his talent that he paid for William to study in Paris, France. In the 1920s, every painter wanted to study in Paris, which was full of artists. William arrived there in 1926, and soon he met Henry Ossawa Tanner, the famous African-American painter. The next year, William had his first exhibition of paintings. It was held at the Students and Artists Club in Paris.

In 1929, William was back in New York. He exhibited his work at the Harmon Foundation and won first prize. Over the years, the Harmon Foundation acquired many more of William's pictures. By 1967, it had collected more than a thousand of his paintings, which are now in the National Museum of American Art in Washington, D.C.

William married a Danish artist in 1930 and moved to a fishing village in Denmark. Throughout the 1930s, he constantly changed his style of painting. He was influenced by the European countries he visited as well as by the artists under whom he trained.

Personality Profile

Career: Painter.

Born: March 18, 1901, in Florence, South Carolina, to Henry and Alice Johnson.

Died: April 13, 1970, on Long Island, New York.

Education: National Academy of Design; Cape Cod School of Art; studied art in Paris, France.

Awards: National Academy of Design's Cannon Prize, 1924; School Prize and Hallgarten Prize, 1925-26; Harmon Foundation's gold medal, 1929.

By 1938, when William again returned to New York, he had developed his own bold style. It was especially suited to the scenes of African-American life he was now painting.

William remained in New York during World War II. During these years, he produced hundreds of superb paintings. Some were illustrations of well-known spirituals such as "Swing Low, Sweet Chariot." Others were pictures of Bible stories in which all people were black. Many were paintings of everyday life, showing people at work and in their leisure hours. Some were set in Harlem, while others showed the South Carolina countryside where William was raised.

Unfortunately, this was to be William's last great burst of painting. His wife died in 1943, and three years later he was found to have a rare form of paralysis. He spent his last twenty-three years in a hospital and never painted again.

Accomplishments

1927 First one-person show in Paris, France.

1928 One-person show in Nice, France.

1929 Exhibited at the Harmon Foundation, New York.

1930 Exhibition in South Carolina.

1939 Painted *Nativity* and *Descent from the Cross*. His painting *Chain Gang* was exhibited at New York's World's Fair.

Paul Robeson

T he youngest in his family, Paul was the only child still at home when his mother died. He was six years old. Paul's father, a Methodist minister, took him to live in Somerville, New Jersey. Paul's father was a courageous man who had started life as a slave and had escaped. He taught Paul to be fearless and to do what was right. As well, he always encouraged Paul to work hard and do his best.

Paul was an excellent student. After graduating from high school, he won a scholarship to Rutgers College. Paul was the only black student at Rutgers, and when he was picked for the football team, the other players threatened to quit. They changed their minds when Paul became their star player. He was also good at other sports and became extremely popular. When, in 1920, he enrolled at Columbia University in New York City to study law, his weekend games of professional football paid for his studies.

Paul was the only black student at Rutgers, and when he was picked for the football team, the others threatened to quit.

55

While Paul was at Columbia, he acted in a play put on by some friends. He did it just for fun and did not plan to be an actor. He performed so well, however, that he was persuaded to take the lead role in a professional play called *Voodoo*. After a successful run in New York, the play went on tour to Britain.

When Paul returned from Britain, he completed his law training and joined a law firm in New York City. This was not a success. Some of the white staff treated him rudely, and Paul could not get much work as a young, black lawyer. At the same time, he was offered many acting roles.

By 1924, Paul had given up all thought of being a lawyer. He starred in two plays, *The Emperor Jones* and *All God's Chillun Got Wings*. Both brought him great praise and led to more roles, including parts in movies. Meanwhile, Paul was also becoming famous as a concert singer. In 1925, he set off on a concert tour that took him through the United States and then across the Atlantic to Europe. His deep, rich voice seemed especially suited to the spirituals he sang. From then on, Paul spent much of his time in Europe. In 1930, he was a great success playing the lead role in Shakespeare's *Othello* in England. Othello became one of his most famous roles.

Personality Profile

Career: Singer and actor.

Born: April 9, 1898, in Princeton, New Jersey, to William and Anna Robeson.

Died: January 23, 1976, in Philadelphia, Pennsylvania.

Education: B.A., Rutgers College, 1919; LL.B., Columbia University, 1923.

Awards: Donaldson Award, 1944; National Medal of Arts, 1944; Spingarn Medal, National Association for the Advancement of Colored People (NAACP), 1945; Champion of African Freedom Award, National Church of Nigeria, 1950; Stalin Peace Prize, 1952; Civil Liberties Award, 1970; Duke Ellington Medal, Yale University, 1972; numerous other awards and several honorary degrees.

In 1934, Paul made his first visit to the Soviet Union. He was delighted with the country because there seemed to be no racism. Paul sent his son to school there so that the boy could grow up free from racial prejudice. Paul believed that the Soviet system was fairer than the American system.

Paul's admiration for the Soviets caused him great trouble after World War II when the United States became very anti-communist. Paul was labeled a communist, and the government took away his passport in 1950. For eight years, Paul could not travel outside the United States. Because of his political views, he found it almost impossible to find work. Theater and movie directors did not employ him, and stores would not sell his records.

When Paul regained his passport in 1958, he went to England. But his career was over. He performed very little in the years before his death in 1976.

Accomplishments

1922 Played the lead role in *Voodoo*.

1923 Received his law degree and became a lawyer.

1924 Was star of *The Emperor Jones* and *All God's Chillun Got Wings*.

1925 Held his first major concert in New York.

1926 Set off on a concert tour of Europe.

1936 Starred in the movie of the musical *Show Boat*.

1943 Starred in Shakespeare's *Othello* in New York.

1944 Made a coast-to-coast tour of the United States.

1958 Gave a farewell concert at Carnegie Hall, New York City, New York.

1973 Seventy-fifth birthday party organized at Carnegie Hall.

Jackie Torrence

Jackie spent her first years with her grandparents in the small farming community of Second Creek, North Carolina. She loved to curl up in a corner and listen to her grandparents' stories. Her grandfather would sit in his comfortable rocker while her grandmother baked bread at the wood stove. Jackie would be in her favorite corner—but in her mind she was far away, caught up in the adventures her grandparents were describing.

They were very happy years, and Jackie remembers them fondly. It was a sad day for her when she reached school age and was sent to live with an aunt in Salisbury, the nearest town. Jackie was lonely there. She had no friends in Salisbury, and she was teased at school.

Jackie had a speech problem: "Whenever I began to talk, it sounded as though I had rocks in my mouth." Jackie found out why she had difficulty speaking only after she was accidentally hit in the mouth with a bottle. The dentist discovered she had a serious dental problem.

With the help of her teachers, Jackie overcame her speech difficulties and shyness. One teacher encouraged her to write stories that the teacher then read to the class. Another teacher taught her to speak clearly. By the time Jackie was a teenager, she was reading from the Bible at her high school assembly. A few years later, when Jackie enrolled at Livingstone College, she felt so confident that she joined the Drama Club and acted in a play.

While still at Livingstone, Jackie married a fellow student. He became a minister, serving a number of churches throughout the southern states in the 1960s. During the eight years of their marriage, Jackie sometimes stood in for him by telling Bible stories to the people at church. But it was after their marriage failed that she really began her career as a storyteller. It happened almost by accident.

Personality Profile

Career: Storyteller.

Born: February 12, 1944, in Chicago, Illinois.

Education: Public schools in Salisbury, North Carolina; Livingstone College.

To earn her living after her marriage broke up, Jackie took a job as a reference librarian in High Point, North Carolina. One day in 1972, the children's librarian became ill. The library director asked Jackie if she would fill in by reading the children a story. She was unwilling at first, but she agreed. She was soon glad she had. The children loved the way Jackie read. They asked for more. That was the moment, Jackie says, when "the bug bit me. I've been in love with storytelling ever since."

Jackie became the library's regular storyteller. Instead of reading stories, she began to tell them from memory. She was such a success that neighboring communities asked her to visit. She became known as "the Story Lady." Some of Jackie's stories were ones she had heard from her grandparents when she was a child. Others, such as the Uncle Remus stories, were well-known children's tales. Many were about African Americans.

Jackie's storytelling took up so much of her time that she left the library and became a full-time storyteller. Since then, Jackie has become well known throughout North America. As well as being a popular performer at festivals, she visits schools and colleges. She performs on television and radio and has toured in Canada and Mexico as well as the United States.

Storytelling is more than a profession for Jackie. She knows she is carrying on an important tradition. "If it had not been for storytelling, the black family would not have survived," she says. In this age of television, Jackie is giving new life to an age-old African-American tradition.

August Wilson

A ugust's first home was a crowded two-room apartment in a black slum in Pittsburgh, Pennsylvania, where he lived with his five brothers and sisters. August's mother struggled to support her children by working as a cleaner. The children hardly ever saw their father. He was a German baker, and he did not live with the family.

When August was a teenager, his mother married an African American. The family moved to a much nicer home in a white neighborhood. August and his family were not welcomed by their new neighbors. Bricks were thrown through their window. August was hassled so much by the white students that he dropped out of school when he was fifteen.

August and his family were not welcomed by their new neighbors. Bricks were thrown through their window.

Although August had left school, he had not finished his education. He had always enjoyed reading, and now he read more eagerly than ever. He spent much of his time at the public library, studying the works of African-American writers. August hoped to be a writer like them.

August dates his life as a writer from April 1, 1965. That was when he bought his first typewriter. He bought it with the twenty dollars his sister had given him for writing a term paper for her. At first, he wrote mainly poetry and a few short stories. Then he tried his hand at plays. Meanwhile, he earned his living by taking odd jobs. For a while, he worked as a cook in a coffee shop.

In 1968, August and a friend formed the Black Horizons Theater Company that put on his first plays. Later, other companies also staged his works.

August's first big success was a play about the blues singer Ma Rainie. It was called *Ma Rainie's Black Bottom*. Black bottom was the name of a dance that was popular in Ma Rainie's day. The play was first staged in 1984 in New Haven, Connecticut. It did so well that it was soon moved to Broadway in New York. It won several awards, including the New York Drama Critics' Circle award.

The critics raved about August. They called him a major new playwright. He proved them right in 1985 with his next play, *Fences*. It won the Pulitzer Prize for drama as well as many other awards. *Fences* is about a father's relationship with his son. The father had been a baseball star in the days when African Americans could not play in the major leagues. The father is so angry about the unfairness of this that he will not let his son accept an athletic scholarship.

Many of August's plays express anger. Most are about the problems of African Americans. *The Piano Lesson*, which was staged on Broadway in 1990, is about a brother and sister who quarrel over whether or not to sell their family's piano. The brother wants money to buy land, and the sister wants the piano as a family treasure.

August's later plays have continued to win awards and to get rave reviews. As the reviewers point out, his plays give a superb picture of African-American life. August says that "black Americans have the most dramatic story of all mankind to tell." With each new play he writes, August reveals a bit more of this dramatic story.

Accomplishments

1968 Founded Black Horizons Theater Company.

1979 Staged *The Homecoming*, his first major play.

1984 Staged *Ma Rainie's Black Bottom*.

1985 First performance of *Fences*.

1987 Won Pulitzer Prize for *Fences*.

1990 Won Pulitzer Prize for *The Piano Lesson*.

Index

1 2 3 4 5 6 7 8 9 0 Printed in Canada 6 5 4 3 2 1 0 9 8 7